GERARDUS
MERCATOR

FATHER OF MODERN MAPMAKING

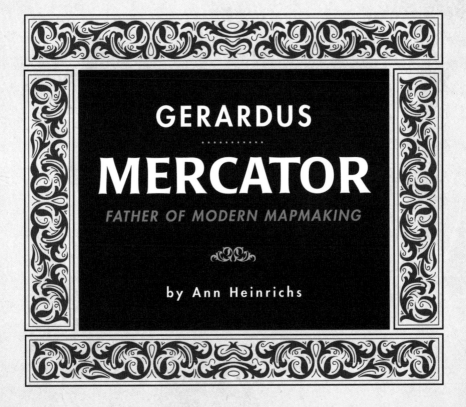

GERARDUS
MERCATOR
FATHER OF MODERN MAPMAKING

by Ann Heinrichs

Content Adviser: Robert W. Karrow Jr.,
Curator of Maps, The Newberry Library

Reading Adviser: Rosemary G. Palmer, Ph.D.,
Department of Literacy, College of Education,
Boise State University

Compass Point Books ✦ Minneapolis, Minnesota

Compass Point Books
3109 West 50th Street, #115
Minneapolis, MN 55410

Visit Compass Point Books on the Internet at *www.compasspointbooks.com*
or e-mail your request to *custserv@compasspointbooks.com*

Editor: Jennifer VanVoorst
Page Production: Bobbie Nuytten
Photo Researcher: Svetlana Zhurkin
Cartographer: XNR Productions, Inc.
Library Consultant: Kathleen Baxter

Art Director: Jaime Martens
Creative Director: Keith Griffin
Editorial Director: Nick Healy
Managing Editor: Catherine Neitge

Library of Congress Cataloging-in-Publication Data
Heinrichs, Ann.
  Gerardus Mercator : father of modern mapmaking / by Ann R. Heinrichs.
     p. cm. — (Signature lives)
  Includes bibliographical references.
  ISBN-13: 978-0-7565-3312-0 (library binding)
  ISBN-10: 0-7565-3312-0 (library binding)
  1. Mercator, Gerhard, 1512–1594—Juvenile literature. 2. Cartographers—
  Netherlands—Biography—Juvenile literature. I. Title. II. Series.
  GA923.5.M5H45 2008
  526.092—dc22
  [B]   2007004902

Signature Lives

SCIENTIFIC REVOLUTION

The Scientific Revolution was a period of radical change in basic beliefs, thoughts, and ideas. Most historians agree that it began in Europe about 1550 with the publication of Nicolaus Copernicus' astronomical theories about Earth and its place in the universe. It ended about 1700 with the landmark work of Isaac Newton and his resulting universal laws. During those 150 years, ideas about astronomy, biology, and physics, and the very way scientists worked, underwent a grand transformation.

Table of Contents

ATIS · *Mercator, tractusque noúos, terraque, marisque* · SVÆ

...tem superasse laborem, · *Mons*

...bona · *ludet.*

Polus uec

Antarcticus

GERARDI MERCATORIS RVPELMVNDANI EFFIGIEM ANNO
DVORVM ET SEX — AGINTA, SVI ERGA IPSVM STVDII
CAVSA DEPINGI CVRABAT FRANC. HOG. CIƆ IƆ LXXIV.

1 BEHIND PRISON WALLS

❧❧❧

One crisp winter day in 1544, Gerardus Mercator strolled down the winding lanes of his boyhood home. It was the village of Rupelmonde in Flanders—now a part of Belgium. Suddenly, soldiers grasped him by the arms. As they marched him through town, old friends and neighbors looked on with dismay.

At last they reached the foreboding tower of Rupelmonde Castle. Surly guards threw Mercator into a cold, dark cell. Then the door slammed shut.

Huddled within the damp, gray walls of the castle prison, he tried to make sense of what had happened. Just days before, he had left his wife and children behind for a short trip to Rupelmonde. A hardworking family man, he was a maker of maps and globes. According to his friend and neighbor Walter Ghim,

In 1574, Franz Hogenberg engraved a portrait of Flemish cartographer Gerardus Mercator.

he was a man of fine character, too:

> *Wherever he lived, he always got on well*
> *with his neighbours; he crossed nobody's*
> *path; had proper regard to the interests*
> *of others; and did not put himself over*
> *anyone else.*

In the darkness Mercator could hear the shrieks and wails of other prisoners, some of whom would likely be put to death. He shuddered to think what could happen to him. What would become of his family? And why was he here in the first place?

A 19th-century illustration from John Foxe's The Book of Martyrs *shows heretics being tortured.*

What Mercator didn't know at the time was that he had been arrested for heresy, a charge that had both religious and political foundations. He lived during a turbulent period in European history. The

Middle Ages, or medieval times, were drawing to a close. This had been a time of looking inward toward spiritual concerns. Christianity had spread across the land, unifying people with common beliefs and values.

During the Middle Ages, the Roman Catholic Church was the only Christian faith in Europe. Religion and politics went hand in hand. Catholic kings and princes ruled, and church leaders played a strong role in government. For peasants and towns-people alike, daily life centered on church services and the year's religious feast days. Children learned the Bible and other religious teachings from the parish priest. Medieval maps reflected religious beliefs, too. The holy city of Jerusalem was considered the center of the world, and Earth was the center of the universe.

At the same time, a new outlook was taking hold in Europe. The period known as the Renaissance was blossoming. Renaissance means "rebirth," and this period ushered in many new ideas. The Renaissance was a time of looking outward and exploring. Navigators were venturing far across the seas into unknown lands. The printing press had been invented in the 1400s, too, and now people could read about the latest advances in science, medicine, geography, and astronomy. Armed with new knowledge, people began to question their old beliefs.

These new ways of thinking alarmed the Catholic Church. Many new ideas were labeled as heresy—false beliefs that departed from church teachings. Religious and political leaders joined forces to stamp out forbidden ideas. The penalty for heresy could be imprisonment or even death.

Mercator was imprisoned for heresy. Yet all his life he had tried to serve God faithfully. He had served worldly rulers as well. Already he had made maps and globes for some of the most powerful leaders in Europe. Surely he wondered where he had gone wrong.

Mercator would never really know. Neither could he foresee what his future held. Mercator was destined to be one of the most famous mapmakers in history. Before his time, many maps were as much about myths as geographical reality, filled with exotic creatures and fabled lands. But he turned cartography, or mapmaking, into a science. He based his maps on firsthand reports, using

Mercator lived during a time period known as the Age of Exploration, or the Age of Discovery. During this time, rulers of many European nations sent ships out to sea. They hoped to expand their domains and find new trade routes to the rich lands of Asia. In 1487, Bartolomeu Dias of Portugal rounded the southern tip of Africa. In 1492, just 20 years before Mercator's birth, Christopher Columbus made his first voyage from Spain to the New World. In 1522, when Mercator was 10, Ferdinand Magellan's Spanish expedition completed the first voyage around the world. Such explorations created a demand for new and better maps.

mathematical calculations whenever possible to pinpoint locations.

Navigators such as Ferdinand Magellan suffered from the lack of accurate maps to plan their voyages.

As Mercator languished in his cell, his greatest work was yet to come. Navigators were sailing across thousands of miles of ocean. But their maps were faulty, and they often ended up far off course. Mercator puzzled over this problem for years.

At last he devised a way to take a round object— Earth—and fit it onto a flat map for dependable navigation. That style of map was named the Mercator projection. For his many accomplishments, Mercator would be remembered as the father of modern mapmaking.

All that was far in the future, though. At the moment, things looked hopeless. For all he knew, this could be the end of his career—and the end of his life. ᴥ

2 DAYS OF HUNGER

❧⦿❧

Gerardus Mercator the mapmaker began his life in a humble farming community. Before he was born, his parents, Hubert and Emerentia Kremer, lived in Gangelt, a village in the duchy of Jülich. A duchy was a region ruled by a duke. Today this region straddles the border between Germany and the Netherlands.

The Kremers scratched out a meager living from the soil. But in the summer of 1511, a drought laid waste to the crops. With six children to feed and another one on the way, the Kremers were desperate. With little to eat, they needed a safe, comfortable place to spend the harsh winter months. So they packed up their family and moved. Their destination was Rupelmonde in Flanders—several days' journey away.

Flemish painter Joachim Beuckelaer depicted a 16th-century country market.

In Mercator's time, Flanders was an important county in the Low Countries. The Low Countries were a broad region of low-lying land in northern Europe that lay where the Scheldt, Maas, and Rhine rivers flow into the North Sea. This region bustled with trade. Ships from all over the world pulled into their ports. Many cities had flourishing manufacturing industries, too.

Rupelmonde lay on the banks of the Scheldt River, just upstream from the busy city of Antwerp. Hubert's brother Gisbert was a priest there, serving as the chaplain at Rupelmonde's hospice of St. Johann. At the time, a hospice was a place where weary travelers could find food, shelter, and rest.

Gisbert welcomed his relatives and showed them to a tiny guesthouse. It was there that, at 6 A.M. on March 5, 1512, the Kremers' youngest child was born. Named Gerard, this child would later be known as Gerardus Mercator.

When the winter snows began to melt, the family returned to Gangelt. Hubert and Emerentia tried to find new ways to make a living. Hubert made extra money by working as a shoemaker. Even so, the Kremers struggled to keep food on the table. Often they had only bread to eat, and they rarely could afford to eat meat.

Finally the Kremers faced the fact that they could not make a living in Gangelt. They needed to live somewhere else. The obvious choice was Rupelmonde, where Hubert's kindly brother lived. So in 1518, when Gerard was 6, the family moved to Rupelmonde to begin a new life.

Shortly after they arrived, Gerard and his older brothers began attending school. Their Uncle Gisbert no doubt kept a watchful eye on his nephews' education. As a devout Catholic priest, he hoped one of the Kremer boys might choose a life in the priesthood.

In Rupelmonde's village school, Gerard studied arithmetic and religion. In addition, he studied Latin,

Rupelmonde Castle is the centerpiece of Mercator's hometown.

the official language of the Catholic Church. Latin was also the language of learning, used by universities and scholars of the time. Lawyers, scientists, and doctors all wrote their official documents in Latin. Gerard learned his lessons well. By the time he was 7 years old, he could read and speak Latin fluently.

Meanwhile, in the outside world, drastic changes were brewing. Here and there, people were growing discontented with the Catholic Church. Some felt that church leaders were greedy, corrupt, and too powerful. Others doubted the church's teachings. A German priest named Martin Luther began publicly criticizing the church. In 1517 Luther nailed his *Ninety-five Theses* on a church door in Wittenburg, Germany. The document was a list of complaints against the Catholic Church. This began a movement of protest and reform called the Protestant Reformation. The church tried to stop the growing influence of Luther's teachings and eventually condemned him as a heretic. He was excommunicated, or expelled from the church, in 1521. Thanks to the printing press, however, Luther's message spread across Europe, and within a few decades, many people in Europe converted to Protestantism.

During this time of tumult, Gerard's father died. It was 1526, and Gerard was only 14 years old. This was a devastating blow. What would become of him without the family breadwinner? His mother,

Martin Luther translates the Bible at Wartburg Castle in an 1898 painting by Eugene Siberdt.

Emerentia, could scrape by on the savings Hubert left behind, and his siblings were now young adults who could fend for themselves. Would Gerard have to give up his schooling and go to work, too?

Fortunately, Uncle Gisbert stepped in. He took the boy under his wing and became his guardian. Gerard moved in with his uncle, who fed, clothed, and taught him. But Gisbert could see that Gerard needed a much better education than he could provide. The boy had done well at Rupelmonde's little school. With his skills, he could perhaps hope to be a merchant's assistant or a clerk. But Gisbert wanted the best for his nephew, so in 1527, he sent Gerard off on a journey into the unknown. ☙

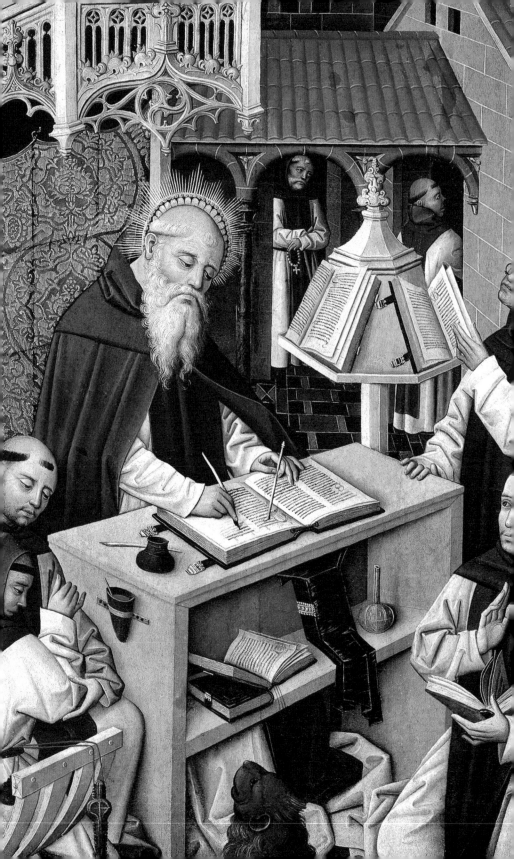

3 LEAVING HOME

❧❦❧

Gerard Kremer must have been excited as he set off on his new adventure. His uncle had chosen a school for him in the town of 's-Hertogenbosch, Dutch for "The Duke's Woods," in the duchy of Brabant. At the time, this was the second-largest city in what is now the Netherlands. Still, the 15-year-old must have been sad to leave his mother. Would he ever see her again? And surely he would miss his uncle and the little village where he had spent his childhood days.

With his few belongings tied up in a pack, Gerard set out on the dusty road. It would be a five-day journey by foot. Probably he joined other travelers, such as merchants or students. Weary peasants trudged along, too, headed for market towns. On the way, Gerard crossed sandy wastelands

A 16th-century painting shows the interior of a scriptorium school, where religious men painstakingly hand-copied religious texts in flowing script.

and trickling streams and passed fields of grain and grassy meadows with grazing sheep. At last, beyond a soggy swamp, he spied the high stone walls of 's-Hertogenbosch.

The city had been built more than 400 years earlier as a fortress town. Its walls protected citizens from thieves and hostile armies. For added protection, a deep, water-filled moat had been dug outside the walls. About 15,000 people lived within the city walls. High above them rose the tall spire of Saint John's Cathedral.

Gerard made his way through the narrow, winding streets of 's-Hertogenbosch. Past the bustling marketplace, he wandered on toward the poorer section of town. Finally he reached the school and its *domus pauperum scolarium*—Latin for "poor students' house." This would be his home for the next three years.

Gerard's new school was run by the Brethren of the Common Life, a religious community of men dedicated to teaching. Though they were not priests, the Brethren followed strict religious rules. They owned no property and drank no alcohol. Wearing drab gray robes, they led simple lives of work and prayer.

More than 1,000 students were enrolled in the Brethren's school. They lived in several dormitories, according to their level of wealth or poverty. The Brethren were especially devoted to educating

A 1530 painting shows the bustling cloth market in 's-Hertogenbosch.

boys from poor families for the priesthood. For poor boys like Gerard, this was a wonderful chance to get an education.

School life for Gerard was somber and strict. He and the other boys rose before 6 A.M. and donned gray, hooded robes. Then they hurried through the lanes into the center of town. There, in the shadow of the great cathedral, they studied at the city's Latin

In Mercator's time, many schools were run by the church, and only boys were allowed to attend.

school. Back at the Brethren house, they took more classes until 6 P.M. They also attended Mass, the Catholic worship service, twice a day.

Now that he lived in the world of scholars, Gerard had to speak as a scholar. All his classes were conducted in Latin. The Latin school embraced the principles of humanism, a philosophy that favors learning by observation and logic rather than accepting information based on faith. Gerard took classes in grammar, logic, and rhetoric, or persuasive speech. He also studied works by the ancient Greeks and Romans, including the poet Homer, the philosopher Aristotle, and the geographer Ptolemy.

Geography sparked a keen curiosity in Gerard. He later wrote: "Since my youth, geography has been for me the primary object of study." The work of Ptolemy surely inspired Gerard as well. Ptolemy was one of the greatest astronomers and geographers of the ancient world. He worked in Alexandria, Egypt, a center of Greek culture and learning. In his

During the Renaissance, ancient Greek and Roman writings were rediscovered, having been all but lost during the Middle Ages. This brought about the humanist trend in education. Humanists insisted that people could arrive at the truth through reason. One of the most prominent humanists was Desiderius Erasmus (c. 1469–1536), who had been both a student and a teacher with the Brethren of the Common Life. His ideas set the stage for the Protestant Reformation.

Geographia he brought together all the geographic knowledge of his time. He included maps showing all the regions of the world he knew. Ptolemy devised the method of drawing maps with vertical and horizontal lines to establish locations. These lines of longitude and latitude are still used on maps and globes today. In 1406 Ptolemy's *Geographia* was translated from Greek into Latin and became available to scholars throughout Europe. As a result his maps became the model for mapmakers. Later in life Gerard himself would publish a version of Ptolemy's ancient maps.

Gerard's studies at the Brethren's school were quite different. The Brethren were known for making handwritten religious books. For hundreds of years the only way to make new books was to copy them by hand, letter by letter. The Brethren earned income by copying Bibles, prayer books, and other texts. Once the printing press was invented in 1455, books could be printed mechanically. But there was still a demand for beautifully handwritten books. Thus penmanship was an important course of study at the school.

Day after day, in the cool silence of the schoolroom, Gerard practiced his letters, doing his best to make them accurately. He learned both the rounded Roman script and the heavier, more squarish Gothic lettering. Gerard especially loved the

A 1584 woodcut depicts Ptolemy (c. 90–c. 168), the famous Alexandrian astronomer, mathematician, and geographer.

graceful, slanted curves of the italic style. Besides its elegant look, it was easy to read. Later he would choose italic as the best script for maps.

While he was in 's-Hertogenbosch, Gerard received word that his mother had died. Now, at 18 years old, he was an orphan. Except for his relationship with Uncle Gisbert, he had few ties to his background. With his course of study at the Brethren's school drawing to a close, the time was ripe for some changes.

Ptolemy's world map was published in a Latin edition of Geographia *in 1482.*

Uncle Gisbert arranged for Gerard to enroll in the University of Louvain, a famous school in present-day Belgium that still exists today. There he would be back in familiar territory. Louvain lay less than 40 miles (64 kilometers) from Rupelmonde.

At the time, it was the custom for university scholars to take on a Latin name. After all, their classes, books, writings, and even conversations were conducted in Latin. Some students translated their personal names into Latin, while others simply picked a Latin name that fit their outlook on life.

Gerard made an interesting choice. His family name, Kremer, was German for "merchant." That same word in Latin was *merca-tor*. To his first name, he added the Latin suffix *-us*. As a bow to his childhood home, he added a Latin version of Rupelmonde at the end. Thus Gerard Kremer of Rupelmonde became Gerardus Mercator Rupelmundanus. ℰ

The University of Louvain was founded in 1425, making it one of the world's oldest universities. Today the university, called Catholic University of Louvain, is actually two separate schools. In 1970, the university split in two, creating the French-speaking Université Catholique de Louvain, and the Dutch-speaking Katholieke Universiteit Leuven.

4 UNIVERSITY LIFE

ᴄᴏ⟨✕⟩ᴏ

On August 29, 1530, 18-year-old Gerardus Mercator knelt before Pierre de Corte with his hands clasped in prayer. De Corte was the rector, or highest official, of the University of Louvain. Dressed in a purple robe, he led the solemn ceremony for new students. Mercator devoutly swore to obey the university's rules. After confirming his familiarity with Latin and paying his registration fee, he was officially enrolled as a university student.

Students at the University of Louvain lived and studied at several college houses around the city. Mercator's house was known as Castle College, described as the university's "leading and most distinguished school." There he would pursue a two-year master's degree. If he did well, he could go on to study for a doctoral degree.

Mercator registered as one of the *pauperes*—the poor students. Both rich and poor students attended the university. They all wore the same plain bonnets and ankle-length gowns, so they looked alike. But wealthy students lived in private rooms, while students like Mercator slept in dormitories. And though everyone ate in the same dining hall, rich students sat in front, while poor students sat at the far end.

Student life at the university was strict. From dawn till dusk, all activities were governed by rules. First came early morning Mass, followed by breakfast. Next were classes, lunch, and a rest period. Then came more classes, study time, dinner, and bed.

Mercator's classes were conducted in Latin, as they had been at 's-Hertogenbosch. Here, too, he studied the ancient Greeks and Romans, whose writings were the authorities on almost every subject. Mercator pored over these ancient works on subjects such as logic, mathematics, physics, and metaphysics, the study of the nature of the world.

One of Mercator's favorite teachers was Gemma Frisius, a mathematician who was also an expert in medicine, astronomy, geography, and mapmaking. Like Mercator, Frisius had come from a poor family. He was only four years older than Mercator, but he had already published a book on astronomy and geography and was known throughout Europe.

Mercator liked Frisius' approach to science. Frisius honored the knowledge of the ancients, but at the same time, he used up-to-date information, making new calculations based on his own observations. Frisius' classes stirred young Mercator's imagination. Some other classes troubled him, though. Studying the ancient Greek philosopher Aristotle made him especially uneasy.

Gemma Frisius (1508–1555)

Aristotle was one of the greatest thinkers of the ancient world. Known as "the master of those who know," he wrote many books covering history, logic, politics, science, and metaphysics. Aristotle's writings helped form the foundations of Western thought, and his works were the authority on logic, science, the nature of the world, and the makeup of the universe. For Aristotle, Earth was the center of the universe, and the heavens revolved around it. As one moved outward from Earth, one came closer to the "prime mover," the force that kept the system going. Aristotle envisioned heavenly matter—the moon, sun, planets, and stars—as being "purer," or more worthy, than Earth and its inhabitants.

This fit well with the church's view of the relationship between the heavens and Earth. In the Middle Ages, the theologian Thomas Aquinas tried to blend the ideas of the Catholic Church with the teachings of Aristotle. Aquinas' efforts were successful, and Aristotle gained the church's stamp of approval. Anyone who challenged Aristotle's teachings risked being branded a heretic. Not

Aristotle (384–322 B.C.) is one of the most famous ancient Greek philosopher-scientists.

surprisingly, his teachings were a particular target of the Protestant Reformation. Martin Luther challenged Aristotle's dominant position when he claimed, "Aristotle is going downhill, and perhaps he will go all the way down into hell."

At this time most universities existed under the guidance of the Catholic Church. Universities could not teach anything that contradicted church beliefs. The humanist movement, which was more inclined to view man as noble rather than tainted by sin, was on the rise, so universities walked a fine line: They taught science, philosophy, and other humanist subjects, but at the same time, they had to uphold church teachings.

The University of Louvain kept in line with the church and held Aristotle in high regard. In fact, a university rule clearly stated its stance:

> *You will uphold the teaching of Aristotle, except in cases which are contrary to faith. ... No-one will be allowed to reject the opinion of Aristotle as heretical ... unless it has previously been declared heretical by the Faculty of Theology.*

The university was serious. It had once fired a faculty member for doubting Aristotle. Before he was allowed to resume his position, the teacher had to make a public declaration of Aristotle's merits and had to admit that he himself had spoken foolishly.

Mercator agonized over Aristotle's writings. According to Aristotle, everything has a cause. All things arise out of something that existed before them. A plant, for instance, grows from a seed, which itself came from another plant.

For Mercator, however, this doctrine clashed with his own beliefs. He knew the Bible's book of

An illustration made from a medieval engraving shows university students at their studies.

Genesis, which said that God created the world and all things in it from nothing. The first plants and animals were created outright, by an act of God, and could not have come from earlier objects. Years later, he would write:

> *But when I saw that Moses' version of the Genesis of the world did not fit sufficiently in many ways with Aristotle and the rest of the philosophers, I began to have doubts about the truth of all philosophers.*

Mercator believed that the Bible itself proved Aristotle wrong.

Some teachers suspected that Mercator held dangerous views and tried to coax him into writing out his arguments. But he could not speak out against Aristotle, for if he did, he would be accused of heresy and expelled from the university. So Mercator kept his thoughts to himself.

In 1532, after two years of study, Mercator received his master's degree. The next step would be to enter the university's doctoral program, but the 20-year-old felt he could not go on. More schooling only meant more studies that would leave him worried and confused. He had to find a way to reconcile the word of God with the writings of the ancient philosophers. To work this out, he set off on his own journey of discovery. ஒ

5 SETTLING PROBLEMS, LEARNING A TRADE

❧❀❧

Now free of the university, Mercator could think freely, too. He began studying philosophy on his own. He also took trips, wandering alone to other cities. One destination was Antwerp. This lively port city lay near the mouth of the Scheldt River. Ships from England, Italy, Portugal, and Spain docked at its harbor. Along the waterfront, porters scurried by, laden with packs of spices, wine, and other imported goods.

More than 50,000 people lived in Antwerp then. Both residents and foreigners crowded the busy market square. The winding cobblestone streets bristled with shops and craft studios. Printing was one of Antwerp's flourishing industries, and printers, bookbinders, and booksellers all enjoyed

Today, the cathedral and Groote Market in Antwerp, Belgium, look much as they did in Mercator's time.

thriving businesses. Mapmakers took advantage of the city's printing trade. Using reports from travelers and explorers, they turned that information into printed maps.

Mercator must have found Antwerp exciting. He had heard of the sailing ships that plied the distant seas. Now he was seeing these ships for himself. His teacher Frisius had sparked his interest in mapmaking, and now he was exploring one of Europe's great mapmaking centers.

Mercator probably spent time in the town of Mechelen, too. It lay about halfway between Antwerp and Louvain. Mechelen was home to a community of monks who lived humble lives of poverty and prayer. They occasionally criticized the Catholic Church, though, which sometimes made them targets of punishment.

One of the monks, Franciscus Monachus, was a geographer and mapmaker. He based his maps on explorers' reports, using careful measurements, and was known as a man who challenged accepted knowledge. To Monachus, some of the ancient Greeks' ideas could no longer be supported, and he found things to criticize in both the philosopher Aristotle and the geographer Ptolemy. Monachus and Mercator became acquainted and in later years exchanged letters.

Mercator never spoke of his time in Mechelen or

Franciscus Monachus highlighted the Western Hemisphere in his 1529 world map.

the conversations he had with Monachus. If it were to be known that he was associating with such a controversial individual, he would be in danger of being punished as a heretic. Still, Mercator must have found it refreshing to share his own ideas with the outspoken monk. He likely found some resolution to his conflicted ideas, too, because in 1534, he ended his wandering and returned to Louvain. It was time to begin a career and get on with his life.

Mercator loved philosophy, but it would take years to qualify as a philosophy teacher. Besides, as his friend and biographer Walter Ghim later said, "it was clear that these studies would not enable him to support a family in the years to come."

Instead, Mercator decided to pursue philosophy in the form of geography. Both religion and philosophy explain the mysteries of the world, but by studying geography, Mercator could approach those mysteries using reason, investigation, measurement, and mathematics, rather than simply relying on faith or beliefs. And it was practical: A geographer could earn a good income making maps and mapping tools.

To work as a geographer, however, Mercator needed to know much more about mathematics, as well as geometry and astronomy. He turned to his old teacher Gemma Frisius, who was happy to let the young man attend his upper-level lectures at the university. Unfortunately, Mercator found he was in over his head. Try as he might, he could not understand the subject matter. Frisius assigned him a reading list to bring him up to speed, and Mercator tore into his studies like a hungry animal. According to one historian, he "drove himself on with relentless concentration, often going without food and sleep."

Frisius was impressed with his young student's progress and soon realized he could use Mercator's skills. Frisius had been working with a goldsmith named Gaspard van der Heyden. The two had a workshop in Louvain where they made maps, globes, and scientific instruments. Frisius invited

Mercator to work there as an apprentice. Flattered, Mercator jumped at the chance to begin his career under such renowned masters.

From van der Heyden, Mercator learned the art of engraving, an essential skill for making printed maps. It required a steady hand, intense concentration, and a flair for art. Mercator practiced hard, learning to cut delicate patterns into copper printing plates.

Mercator also learned to make several kinds of scientific instruments, following Frisius' designs. Day after day, he labored in the workshop—sawing, grinding, and polishing copper and brass. One instrument was the cross-staff. It was a rod with sliding crossbars for observing the stars. Another tool was

Cross-staffs allowed sailors to make measurements based on the stars for use in navigation.

the astrolabe. It was used to find one's location by measuring the positions of the sun and stars. Frisius also designed astronomical rings. They consisted of three brass rings that swiveled inside each other. Engraved on the rings were hours of the day, compass directions, and other measurements. Among other things, they could be used to tell time.

These were all practical instruments used by astronomers, navigators, and surveyors. But they were decorative, too, and wealthy collectors acquired them for their sheer beauty. One avid collector was Emperor Charles V. As head of the Holy Roman Empire, he was the most powerful ruler in Europe. Charles admired Frisius' work, and in 1535, he ordered the workshop to make him a magnificent globe of the world.

Charles V, Holy Roman Emperor (1500–1558)

The three craftsmen mustered their best efforts for this grand project. They proposed to make "a globe or sphere of the whole world, on which the recently discovered islands and lands will be added, and which will be improved and enriched and more beautiful" than any they had made before.

First, they made a sphere out of papier-mâché. To make it stiff and smooth, they covered it with plaster. To cover the globe, the men printed a world map on paper and then pasted it onto the globe. They used the geographical information Frisius had gathered from land and sea explorers. This map was not rectangular. To fit on the round surface, it was made in twelve sections called gores. Each gore was a long strip, fat in the center and pointed on each end. On the globe, the gores would look like sections of a peeled orange.

The entire map, split into gores, was engraved onto copper plates. Besides land and sea, there were place names and explanatory notes. For an artistic touch, the map was adorned with illustrations of sailing ships, sea monsters, and stars. Van der Heyden would engrave the geographical features and decorations, but Mercator was to engrave all the lettering. That consisted of hundreds of tiny place names, as well as the notes.

In Mercator's time, much of central Europe belonged to the Holy Roman Empire. This empire was both a political and a religious union. It was divided into many separate states ruled by dukes, counts, or princes. Over them all reigned the Holy Roman Emperor. The emperors were Roman Catholics who honored the authority of the pope, the head of the Catholic Church. Eventually, however, the Protestant Reformation weakened the empire, and many states became Protestant and opposed the emperor's reign.

Before the mid-1500s, maps had been printed with woodblocks. The images were printed from designs carved onto wood. But most wood was too coarse for carving fine details. A truly useful map had to show rivers, coastlines, and other features as accurately as possible. Place names had to be spelled out in tiny letters. Engravers did this by carving in metal instead of wood. Using a sharp-pointed instrument called a burin, they cut fine lines into a metal such as copper. Ink was then applied to the copper plates to print the maps.

Mercator must have been both terrified and thrilled. This was the biggest challenge he had ever faced in his new profession. And it was for the emperor himself! Through the winter he labored in the workshop, bent over copper plates. All the lettering practice from his school days paid off as he etched out his graceful script.

At last, in 1536, the globe was assembled and mounted on a stand. It measured only about 14½ inches (37 centimeters) across. But it was a splendid globe, one truly fit for an emperor. A note on the globe gave credit to its makers and offered Mercator his first public mention:

Gemma Frisius, doctor and mathematician, described this work from various observations made by geographers and gave it this form. Gerard Mercator of Rupelmonde engraved it with Gaspard van der Heyden, from whom the work, a product of extraordinary cost and no less effort, may be purchased.

A 1598 colored woodcut is the earliest printed picture of a cartographer at work.

Overflowing with well-earned pride, Mercator now felt he had arrived. He had been trained by two of the best craftsmen in Europe, and he had excellent skills. A modern historian described him as having become "a superb engraver, an outstanding calligrapher, and one of the leading scientific instrument makers of his time—all this by the age of 24." It was time for the young geographer to strike out on his own. 🎵

Chapter 6

PUTTING THE WORLD ON PAPER

 formes

In 1536, Gerardus Mercator decided to go into business for himself in Louvain. Little did he know that in doing so he was laying the foundation of his reputation as the foremost geographer of the century.

Gemma Frisius did not mind losing Mercator. He was proud of his young apprentice and wished him well. Besides, there was plenty of business to go around. Orders were streaming in from Antwerp and the surrounding area. Sailors, travelers, and curious citizens needed maps. Doctors, navigators, and astronomers needed scientific instruments. Frisius even lent Mercator some tools and equipment until he could afford to buy his own.

Now that his career was launched, Mercator was in a position to marry. Ten long years had passed

Mercator's 1541 terrestrial globe was one of his great successes.

since he had enjoyed a family life. Now he wanted the rewards and comforts of a family home.

Mercator found the ideal mate in a local girl named Barbara Schelleken. Like Mercator, Barbara had grown up in a large family. She, too, had lost her father at an early age. Since she had helped raise her siblings, Mercator knew Barbara would make a good mother. And she was proficient in the many tasks of running a household. Neighbor Walter Ghim later described her as "a woman of chaste morals, submissive, and an excellent housewife, well suited to his manner of life."

Gerardus and Barbara were married in August 1536. They made their home in St. Pierre's Parish in Louvain. Their little house stood on a street behind a monastery, with Mercator's workshop nearby. Just a year later, their first child was born. Almost every year, the Mercators would welcome a new child to the family until they had six children. They included three sons—Arnold, Bartholomew, and Rumold—and three daughters—Emerentia, Dorothée, and Katharina.

As young Mercator began his new life, Europe was in turmoil. Emperor Charles V was having trouble keeping control of the Holy Roman Empire. The empire's German states resented his authority. Most German princes held more power than Charles did. They collected taxes and built up their own armies.

In addition, Protestantism had gained a foothold in the German states. As a devout Catholic, Charles was alarmed by the spread of Martin Luther's teachings. In 1521 he had issued the Edict of Worms, which declared Luther an outlaw and a heretic. It also outlawed Luther's books and any other writings considered to be heresy.

Charles himself had spent his childhood in the Low Countries, where Mercator lived, and he was determined that this territory not fall to the Protestants. In 1530 Charles put his sister, Queen Mary of Hungary, in charge of the Low Countries. Mary was even more fiercely Catholic than Charles was. She had dozens of people executed for heresy in the 1530s.

Martin Luther appeared before Holy Roman Emperor Charles V at Worms in 1521.

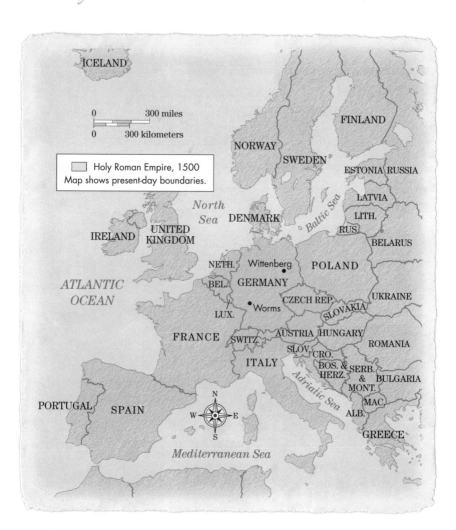

Surely Mercator was aware of these events. Nevertheless, he was busy with his own affairs. The new family man was hard at work in his workshop. He remembered well the poverty and hunger of his childhood. Now with a growing family of his own, he was determined to keep everyone well fed and prosperous.

Making scientific instruments gave Mercator a basic income, but geography and maps were his passion. He was driven to explain the world by putting it down on paper. His religious faith was a strong force, too. Somehow, he hoped he could join the earthly world with the spiritual world through his work.

All his life Mercator had been fascinated with the Bible. The creation story had filled his mind in his student days, and the Bible's book of Exodus intrigued him as well. It told of the Israelites' escape from Egypt to the Promised Land. He decided his first big project would be a map of Palestine. In Mercator's time, Palestine was the name used for the Holy Land—the lands described in the Bible.

A map of Palestine was sure to sell well. The Bible was the one book that ordinary people knew best. With a map of the Holy Land, they could see where biblical events took place as they read about them. Pilgrims visiting the Holy Land could use the map, too.

Mercator studied the Bible carefully so he could put places in their proper locations. Then he decorated the map, using his finest engraving skills. Jagged mountains rose across the landscape. Angels blew winds from the clouds above. Rivers featured gently rippling waves, while ships and fish pitched on rolling seas. Tiny tents showed the Israelites' campsites on their escape from Egypt. Finally he added his graceful lettering.

Mercator made his map easy to use. He printed it on six separate sheets of paper that fit neatly into a packet. They could be pasted together to make a wall map. Published in 1537, Mercator's Palestine map was enormously popular. It was recognized as the standard map of the Holy Land for decades.

Mercator's map of Palestine was large—more than 3 feet (0.9 meters) long. West, with the Mediterranean Sea, is at the top of the map.

Now Mercator was ready to take on the world—mapping it, that is. In 1538, he published his first world map. It was the first map to show both North and South America. He had labored over the problem of projection—how to put the curved Earth on a flat surface. Mapmakers had always struggled with

the projection problem. No projection was perfect. With its curves flattened, Earth was always distorted in some way. It might be shaped like an oval, a diamond, a heart, or a cone. Sizes might be correct, but distances would be wrong. And if the distances were correct, then the shapes of continents might be wrong. There still is no way to make everything right at once—every projection is a compromise. For his map, Mercator chose a double cordiform projection. That is, he split Earth into two heart-shaped sections. This was just one of his many experiments with projections.

Mercator made his next map for political reasons. Ghent, a prosperous city in Flanders, staged a revolt in 1538. The citizens enjoyed a few months of unusual

Mercator created his first map of the world in 1538.

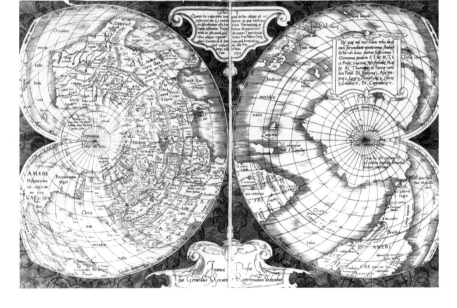

freedom, refusing to pay taxes to the empire. Many people openly defied Catholic doctrine. When they learned the next year that Charles V and his army were coming to Ghent, the emperor's birthplace, they began to regret their actions. Some merchants of Ghent approached Mercator and asked him to make a new map of Flanders that would clearly show that Flanders was loyal to Charles V.

Mercator hastily set to work. His map of 1540 not only featured Charles V's portrait, but it was also dedicated to the emperor. The map may have helped Mercator's own reputation with Charles V, but it did nothing for Ghent. The emperor himself marched in

Originally published in 1540, a reduced-size version of Mercator's map of Flanders appeared in an atlas published by Abraham Ortelius in 1570.

and brutally put down the revolt, destroying large parts of the city in the process.

The next year Mercator made a globe of the world. It was the first globe he had tried since his apprenticeship with Gemma Frisius. By this time, explorers had discovered even more new lands, and Mercator made sure to include them.

Mercator also crisscrossed this globe with rhumb lines—lines drawn across the oceans from one land point to another that show where a ship would sail if it followed its compass on a constant course. Mercator believed the rhumb lines gave navigators valuable information. He hoped he could one day make a flat map that served navigators as well.

Early in 1544 Mercator received some sad news. His dear Uncle Gisbert had died during the winter. Without the kindly old priest's support, Mercator would never have come so far in life. As Gisbert's closest relative, Mercator had to settle his uncle's affairs. So he left Louvain and set out on the road for his boyhood home of Rupelmonde. This journey would lead to the darkest episode of his life. ❧

7 A Most Unjust Persecution

༺∞༻

By the mid-1500s, religious disputes in Europe had built up into a frenzy. Martin Luther's writings had been spreading like wildfire. Other reform movements were springing up, too, challenging the Catholic Church's authority in many areas. Some people refused to accept traditional teachings, while others felt they did not need the church at all, believing that they could reach heaven through faith alone. To the church, these ideas were heresy.

The humanist education system was also under fire. Its method of independent thinking often clashed with church teachings. Even traveling could be a suspicious activity. Someone traveling in Lutheran areas might be picking up heretical ideas.

To stamp out heresy, church leaders established

During the Inquisition, accused heretics were led to prison where they were questioned and sometimes tortured.

the Inquisition, a sort of law-enforcement agency that searched out suspected heretics and arrested them. Inquisition officials questioned and sometimes tortured suspects to obtain confessions. Those who confessed might be given an opportunity to reject their beliefs, or they might be executed regardless. Suspects were compelled to name other supposed heretics, which led to even more arrests. The Inquisition was a widely used abuse of power. Secular rulers—rulers who had no official connection to the church—sometimes used the Inquisition to get rid of political opponents.

In the Low Countries, where Mercator lived, heresy was punished harshly by the Inquisition. The emperor had charged his sister, Queen Mary, with this region, and she ruled with an iron fist. Determined to root out heresy in her domain, she put Pierre Dufief, the attorney general of Brabant, in charge of finding heretics.

Dufief was cruel and ruthless, and he often used torture. He was good at getting people to confess and to name other suspected heretics. Based on his investigations, Dufief drew up a list of suspects. In Louvain alone, he collected 43 names. One of those was Gerardus Mercator. In February 1544, Dufief was ready to swoop through Louvain and make arrests.

Mercator's wife, Barbara, had no idea what was coming. Busy with her household chores, she expected her husband to be back from Rupelmonde any day. Suddenly, Dufief's men pounded on her door. They burst in, demanding to know where Mercator was. Terrified, Barbara told them he was away from home. He had gone to Rupelmonde to oversee his uncle's affairs.

Barbara's answer was not good enough. Authorities believed Mercator knew he was going to be arrested. They believed he had fled to Rupelmonde to hide. Thus he was not only accused of heresy but also considered a fugitive from justice.

Guards searched his house in Louvain from top to bottom. Barbara stood by helplessly as they flung open cabinets and rifled through shelves. They were

During the Inquisition, suspected heretics were sometimes brutally tortured to elicit confessions of heresy.

looking for evidence of Mercator's heresy. That could be Lutheran writings or any other suspicious books or papers. The guards, however, were sorely disappointed: Not a scrap of evidence could be found

Barbara knew her husband was a devoutly religious man. Why had he been arrested? One historian speculated that his "earlier correspondence with [Mechelen], and his more recent absences from Louvain on surveys for his maps, were held against him."

Twelve years earlier, Mercator had visited the monks at Mechelen. They were well known for criticizing the church. Mercator had even exchanged letters with one of the monks. Those letters were suspected of containing heretical ideas. Mercator had also traveled far from home. In making his maps, he sometimes needed to travel to gather geographical information. Perhaps he had gathered dangerous ideas on those trips as well.

Mercator's map of Palestine may also have drawn attention. It was dedicated to Frans van Cranevelt, a scholar and map collector who was well known as a humanist. The map itself may have pointed to Mercator's guilt. It was full of pictures, yet there was no picture of Moses holding the tablets of the Ten Commandments. This could mean that Mercator rejected God's laws—as well as the church.

For whatever reason, Mercator was arrested in Rupelmonde and imprisoned. But why? As far as he knew, he had been living honorably. By this time, his fame as a map and globe maker had spread. His globe of 1541 was selling fast and fetching high prices. Even the emperor was impressed with his work. Mercator had recently received a big order from Charles V. The emperor wanted several globes and scientific instruments for his private collection.

This order was the greatest honor Mercator could imagine. Yet here he was in prison. How could he ever fulfill the emperor's request? And how could his family survive without him? Was it his own fault that he was arrested? Had he been too independent in his thinking? Or maybe others were to blame. Had a friend or neighbor betrayed him? Had someone named him while being tortured? He likely pondered these questions as days and weeks passed.

At home in Louvain, Barbara was worried, too. But unlike Mercator, she could do something about the situation. She went directly to Pierre de Corte, who had been the rector at the University of Louvain when Mercator was enrolled there. Now he was the priest at the Mercators' parish church. Barbara asked him to write a letter on Mercator's behalf. He agreed and wrote to Queen Mary herself:

> *Master Gerard Mercator enjoys a good*
> *reputation. At [Louvain], he leads a reli-*
> *gious and honorable life, and is uncor-*
> *rupted by heresy.*

Queen Mary fired off a letter to de Corte. How did he know Mercator was not a heretic? Furthermore, how could he defend a fugitive? Again de Corte pleaded Mercator's innocence:

> *I would have no wish to excuse [him] if I*
> *knew him to be corrupted by heresy—far*
> *from it, I would know how to carry out my*
> *duty to suppress evil.*

De Corte went on to explain that Mercator was often out of town on business. He was sure that, in leaving Louvain, Mercator "did not quit the town out of fear."

Months passed, and Mercator's case dragged on. Queen Mary decided to send a spy to Mechelen. He was to secretly search for letters that he believed Mercator had written to monks there. But the spy came up empty-handed. Other suspects were questioned about Mercator. Some of them confessed that they had held secret meetings in their homes in which they discussed those church teachings they did not believe. However, not a single person claimed that

Mercator had been present.

Spring and summer came and went, and Mercator continued to languish in jail. He never described his experience in prison. He only called it a "most unjust persecution." However, he undoubtedly continued to be questioned for hours on end. He had nothing to confess, nor could he be tricked into a false con-

Queen Mary of Hungary (1505–1558)

fession. One by one, several other prisoners were executed. Meanwhile, Mercator clung to hope in his dark, damp cell.

Finally, in September 1544, the heavy prison gates swung open, and Mercator emerged a free man. No one knows why he was released. Probably it was because there was no evidence against him. In any case, he was free. After seven months in prison, he was going home at last.

Mercator was overjoyed to see Barbara and his children again. He spent no time relaxing, though. By now, he was behind on all his work. The family finances were badly drained, too. He set to

> *Everything that Mercator made required the carving of letters in metal. The style of lettering he used was the kind of slanted printing that had originated in Italy and that we now call italic. Mercator thought it was the finest and most legible kind of writing—much easier to read than the everyday handwriting used in Germany and the Netherlands. In order to encourage people to learn these letters, he published a book in 1546, showing in detail how to form the letters and even how to hold the pen.*

work at once, finishing Emperor Charles' long-overdue instruments.

The emperor was delighted with Mercator's work. As a reward, he gave Mercator's workshop his official seal of approval. That honor brought even more customers to his door.

In 1551, a letter arrived from Duke Wilhelm of Cleves. The duchy of Cleves was a state in present-day Germany. Duke Wilhelm planned to open a university in the city of Duisburg. He was writing to ask Mercator to come and teach there.

Mercator welcomed this invitation. Duisburg was not far from Gangelt, the village where he had spent the first six years of his life. Even more comforting, Cleves was a Lutheran stronghold. The duke, like other German rulers, had become quite powerful. These rulers were able to protect Lutherans from persecution. Mercator himself did not embrace Lutheranism. But in Cleves he would be safe from charges of heresy.

Mercator gladly accepted Duke Wilhelm's offer.

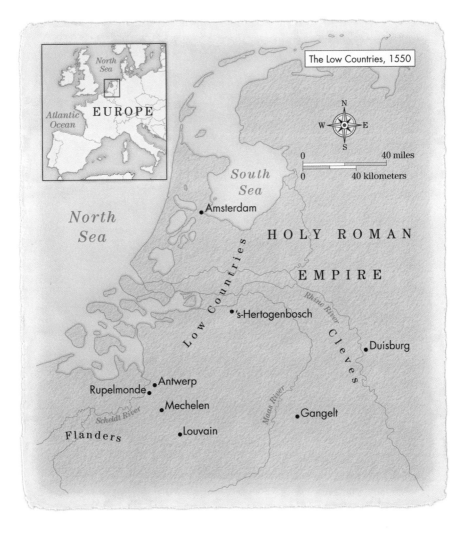

In 1552, he and Barbara rounded up their six children and packed a cart with all their belongings. Then they set out on the road for a days'-long trek to Duisburg. Here Mercator would spend the rest of his life. Here, too, he would create his greatest, most lasting work. ᴥ

In Duisburg, Mercator lived in safer territory and was closer to his childhood home.

8 A History of the Universe

Fewer than 3,000 people lived in Duisburg when the Mercators arrived. Rising high above the city walls was the steeple of the Church of the Savior. Within the city, hundreds of tile-roofed houses lined the narrow streets. Many homes had orchards, gardens, and pens for cattle and pigs.

Gerardus Mercator settled his family into their new home. Once he unpacked his maps, books, and tools, he opened a workshop. Duke Wilhelm's university was still in the planning stages. That meant Mercator would not be teaching right away. However, he had plenty to do.

Emperor Charles had placed another order. This time he wanted a pair of globes, one fitting inside the other. The inner globe was to be Earth. Surrounding it

Gerardus Mercator was named a member of the royal household because of his work for the emperor.

would be a celestial globe—a globe of the heavens.

Mercator applied the most delicate craftsmanship to this exquisite work. Walter Ghim, the mayor of Duisburg, wrote:

> *Shortly after he had made his home among us here, he constructed by order of the Emperor two small globes, one of purest blown crystal and one of wood. On the former, the planets and the more important constellations were engraved with a diamond and inlaid with shining gold; the latter, which was no bigger than the little ball with which boys play in a circle, depicted the world, in so far as its small size permitted, in exact detail.*

Mercator presented the globes to the emperor in person. Charles V rewarded him with the title *Imperatoris domesticus*—"member of the imperial household."

Basking in his new honors, Mercator set to work on his next project. It was a map of Europe. Similar maps existed, but this would outshine them all. To gather information, he examined dozens of earlier maps. He studied explorers' reports and travelers' tales. Ever so carefully, he pinpointed hundreds of towns and land features.

Mercator included so much detail that the map could not fit on one sheet of paper. So he printed it on

Mercator's crystal celestial globe has been lost, but another celestial globe, made in 1551 of papier-mâché, survives. It shows the constellations of the night sky.

15 sheets. When pasted together, in three rows of five sheets, they made a huge wall map. It measured 65 by 53¾ inches (165 by 137 cm). At the time, this was the largest, most accurate map ever made.

Published in 1554, the map assured Mercator's place as Europe's finest mapmaker. Ghim later wrote, "This work attracted more praise from scholars everywhere than any similar geographical work which has ever been brought out."

Orders for the map poured in from all over Europe. With a comfortable income, the Mercators

Originally published in 1554, a reduced-size version of Mercator's map of Europe appeared in his Atlas of 1595.

were able to move into a big house in 1558. The rambling, two-story stone house rose around a courtyard. On one side was the family's residence. Facing it was Mercator's workshop. It was roomy enough to hold his library, as well as workbenches, tables, and equipment. Surrounding the property was a stone fence with an iron gate.

The new house stood on the Oberstrasse, the street where Duisburg's finest citizens lived. Ghim lived there as well, and it was here that the two men became close friends, spending many hours together. Ghim would later write the first biography of Mercator and described his neighbor with admiration and respect:

> He was a man of calm temperament and of exceptional candour and sincerity. He was so fond of peace and tranquility in both public and private affairs that … he never exchanged a harsh word with any of his fellow citizens; he neither entered into any dispute with any man nor was himself summoned to law by anyone.

While waiting for Duke Wilhelm's university to open, Mercator taught mathematics at a Duisburg academy. City records show that one student took two years of instruction there and paid as tuition "three fat piglets."

By 1562, the plans for a university had fallen through. Mercator was disappointed to lose the promise of a comfortable teaching job. Still, he could not complain. His business was thriving, and

Walter Ghim's biography of Mercator, titled Vita Mercatoris, *was published as an essay to accompany the 1595 edition of Mercator's Atlas, which came out after his death. The biography is one of the most important sources of information on Mercator's life and provides dates and details for significant events in Mercator's career. What is left out is significant as well. Ghim makes no mention of Mercator's arrest and imprisonment at the hands of the Inquisition, likely because Mercator himself did not talk about that dark period in his life.*

Cosmography, the study of the heavens and Earth, combines astronomy and geography. In Mercator's time, kings and other rulers often had an official cosmographer who was responsible for making maps based on astronomical observations. With accurate maps, a ruler could know the extent of his domain and determine how much tax landholders had to pay. Maps had a military purpose, too. With an accurate map, a ruler could draw up detailed battle plans. These maps were so valuable that rulers kept them under lock and key.

more honors came his way. In 1564 Duke Wilhelm appointed Mercator as his court cosmographer. In this position, Mercator often traveled to take land measurements for new maps.

Meanwhile, Mercator was hatching plans of his own. He had been mulling over two problems for decades. One was a practical issue: How could he make a reliable map for navigators? But another problem seemed even more crucial. To truly describe what the world looked like, he felt that he needed to be certain of the world's history. He wanted to write a history book, but not an ordinary one. His would be a timeline of the universe, from creation on.

Many histories had been published during the first century of printing, each filled with the dates of various events. The Bible, too, was an important source for much that was known about ancient history. Mercator wanted to bring all this knowledge together, merging biblical history with world history, and correct the dates whenever possible. This would give future historians a firm framework for understanding the past.

Mercator's solution was his *Chronologia*—a timeline for all of history. First, he studied Bible stories carefully. Beginning with the creation of the world, he worked forward in time. Painstakingly, he counted years and calculated time spans.

Next he examined ancient Babylonian, Hebrew, Greek, and Roman calendars. Each one had a different dating system. Using separate columns for each calendar, he matched them with biblical events. Kings, wars, eclipses of the sun and moon—all were given dates.

Mercator was proud of his *Chronologia*. He called it "the complete history of Heaven, Earth and Mankind." Scholars welcomed the massive volume.

As court cosmographer to Duke Wilhelm of Cleves, Mercator's job was to create maps based on astronomical observations.

Mercator's Chronologia gave dates to Bible stories, such as Moses leading the Israelites out of Egypt.

As Ghim wrote:

> *The work so pleased all the most learned men throughout Italy and Germany and*

attracted so much admiration that ...
an Italian of Verona, who was greatly
renowned for his researches into ancient
history ... did not hesitate to rank Mercator
far above all other scientists of note and
many professors of ancient history.

The Catholic Church was not pleased, though. It condemned the *Chronologia* for including events in the Protestant Reformation. Fortunately for Mercator, he was beyond the church's reach. As long as he lived in German territory, he was safe from the danger of arrest.

Within a year, Mercator would produce a bold new invention. It was new kind of map—one that would make his name live on for more than 400 years. ℘

9 Chapter

MAKING THE CURVED EARTH FLAT

In Mercator's time, the most accurate navigators' maps were of the Mediterranean Sea. It was a relatively small sea that had been navigated for thousands of years and mapped for hundreds of years. Out on the wide expanses of the oceans, however, the situation was different. The available maps were not dependable. The directions shown on the navigators' compasses did not fit with their maps. As a result their ships sometimes ran ashore hundreds of miles from where they meant to go. As one historian noted, at that time "navigation was an extremely tricky business—and a risky one too, for many lives were lost due to ships failing to reach their destination."

Navigators tried many tricks to overcome this problem. None were very accurate, though. To sail

A 16th-century engraving by Hieronymus Cock shows geographers taking measurements from a globe.

from Europe to the Caribbean islands, for example, seamen relied on a traditional saying: "Head south until the butter melts, and then turn west."

Mercator wanted to give navigators a reliable map. To do that, he needed to invent a new projection—a new way to represent the curved Earth on a flat map. That would not be easy. He would have to change the mapping system of the ancient Greek geographer Ptolemy.

Ptolemy was the first geographer to draw maps with vertical and horizontal lines (today called lines of longitude and latitude). Until Mercator's time, most mapmakers drew these lines as curved lines. A map projection that uses curved lines for latitude and longitude can make a flat map appear more rounded. It can often make the relative sizes and shapes of landmasses more accurate, too. For this reason, cartographers still make many maps with curved lines of latitude and longitude. But for sailors trying to decide which direction to sail, these kinds of maps simply did not

The north-south lines on a map or globe are called lines of longitude or meridian lines. On a globe, they get closer together as they near the North and South Poles. On world maps, lines of longitude (meridians) are sometimes drawn as curved lines that meet at the poles. The lines of latitude are the east-west lines. On a globe, they make parallel circles around Earth and so are called parallels. The largest circle goes around the equator. As they get closer to the poles, the circles become smaller and smaller. On world maps, lines of latitude (parallels) are sometimes drawn as curved lines.

Sailors used the sun to calculate longitude.

work well. Their compasses could only direct them to sail in straight lines.

On his globe of 1541 Mercator had drawn lines of constant compass direction, or rhumb lines, but these lines were curved on the globe. By following the compass course shown by these curved lines, a navigator could have sailed accurately across an ocean. But a globe was very inconvenient to use aboard a ship, as well as difficult to take measurements from. Besides, to show the kind of detail a navigator would want, the globe would have to be very large and even

> *Navigators decided upon a compass course by looking at flat maps. If their destination was, for example, directly southwest, they followed their compass in that direction. But Mercator knew this created problems when crossing large expanses of ocean. Following a constant, unchanging rhumb line, or compass angle, would not work. Such a course would spiral toward the North or South Pole. Most navigators were not aware of this. They thought they were sailing in a straight line. But they were really sailing on a curved course. Thus they ended up far from their destinations.*

more difficult to use. How could a cartographer make a flat map that would accurately show direction by straight lines? Mercator struggled with this problem day and night.

At last, in 1569, Mercator hit on a solution. He devised a map in which all the curved lines of longitude and latitude were straight. It was as if he had peeled the skin off Earth in one big piece and then stretched the top and bottom of the skin until it lay flat. In order to do this, he gradually increased the distance between the lines of latitude. He also altered the longitude lines. Instead of coming together at the poles, they stayed the same distance apart.

Of course, sizes got distorted in the process. A small country, when "stretched," became a larger country. Distances got distorted, too. A short distance, when "stretched," became a longer distance. Because the lines of latitude and longitude kept spreading out as they neared the poles, lands in the far north and far south looked much bigger than they would on a globe. On Mercator's map, for example, Greenland looks much larger than the continent of South America. In reality, however, it is about one-eighth the size of the continent.

But although areas and distances were exaggerated, especially near the poles, Mercator's new map showed directions correctly. Mercator had accomplished what he had set out to do. He had solved the most serious problem that navigators faced: how to get where they meant to go. Using Mercator's new map, navigators could plot an accurate course. All they had to do was draw a line on the map from one location to another. Then they could follow their compass in that same direction. Instead of sailing off in a curve, they would reach their destination.

Mercator realized his map was highly unusual. He knew it was not accurate for showing sizes and distances. So he was sure to give the map a title to make its purpose clear. He called it "[a] new and more complete representation of the terrestrial globe properly adapted for use in navigation."

Mercator's straight-lined mapping system is called the Mercator projection, or Mercator's projection. This style of map is sometimes called a cylindrical projection. Mercator's new map was the greatest breakthrough in mapmaking history, and it is still used today for navigation of both the oceans and space. In his own time, however, Mercator's map was not popular right away. Navigators did not quite trust it. The unfamiliar shapes and sizes of continents confused them, and they felt safer using their old maps, as troublesome as they were.

Mercator may have drawn his map on a trial-and-error basis by plotting where the rhumb lines on his 1541 globe intersected with coastlines. However he came up with his map, he did not leave instructions for how to space the lines of latitude. In 1599, an English mathematician named Edward Wright corrected this problem and published tables and charts that showed exactly how to change the spacing between the lines

Mercator's 1569 map of the world showcased his innovative projection.

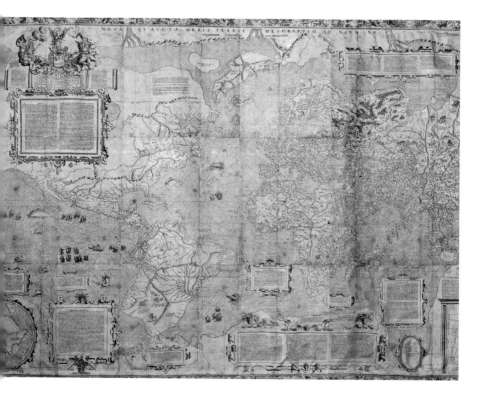

of latitude. With this new information, navigators gradually began to use Mercator's map and to make other maps using the same projection. In 1878, the American Geographical Society noted:

> [I]t is unknown exactly when Mercator's projection was first used. We only know that about the year 1630, the French seaport of Dieppe, on the English Channel, was the principal emporium for the sale of nautical charts, and that those then sold at that place were mostly on this projection.

In time, Mercator's map became the first choice for mariners. It met their needs for an accurate sailing guide. Eventually Mercator-style maps were flying off the printing presses throughout Europe. Even people who were not navigators bought them to hang on their walls. The purpose of the map was easily overlooked.

Nevertheless, Mercator's system remained a valuable mapping tool. Today many agencies use forms of the Mercator projection. They include the U.S. Geological Survey and the National Aeronautics and Space Administration. Their applications range from city maps to the satellite-based global positioning system. ᴥ

ATLAS

SIVE

COSMOGRAPHICÆ

MEDITATIONES

DE

FABRICA MVNDI ET

FABRICATI FIGVRA.

Gerardo Mercatore Rupelmundano,
Illuſtriſſimi Ducis Iuliæ Cliviæ & Mõ
tis &c.ᵒ Coſmographo Autore.
Cum Privilegio.

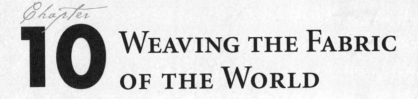

Chapter
10 WEAVING THE FABRIC OF THE WORLD

୬୦୬

Mercator would live for 25 more years after publishing his new map. During that time, he was consumed with grand projects that filled his imagination. Each of these projects took a long time. That was because he had so much ordinary business to handle.

Mercator's workshop was swamped with orders for scientific instruments and copies of earlier maps and globes. His sons Arnold and Rumold had taken over much of the workshop's day-to-day business. Even his grandsons were helping out. Mercator kept an eye on the workshop, making sure all went well. But his mind and heart were elsewhere.

For years, Mercator had dreamed of mapping all the separate regions of the known world. He planned to include Europe, Asia, Africa, and the Americas.

The title page of Mercator's 1595 Atlas *shows Atlas, the mythological figure who inspired the name of the map collection.*

This project was too big to be done with just one huge map. Instead, it would be dozens of separate maps, drawn with precise details. These maps would be bound together in convenient books. Then they would be easier to carry around than globes or wall maps. But first, he had to deal with Ptolemy.

The ancient Greek geographer Ptolemy had also made a set of maps. His *Geographia* contained 27 maps of the world as he knew it. Now, 1,500 years later, much more was known about the world. Ptolemy himself had made mistakes, too. Even more mistakes had crept in as his maps were copied over the centuries. As Mercator said, "In the entire work there is not one part which is not riddled with errors."

Mercator felt he could not proceed with his own map collection until he had fixed Ptolemy's maps. Perhaps this was Mercator's way of honoring his ancient hero. In any case, he corrected Ptolemy's maps and published them in 1578. Then he threw himself into the colossal task ahead.

For his own set of maps, Mercator chose the name *Atlas*. In doing so, he was the first to use this term for a map collection. The work's full name, in Latin, was *Atlas sive Cosmographicae Meditationes de Fabrica Mundi et Fabricati Figura*. That roughly translates as "Atlas, or Cosmographic Meditations on the Fabric of the World and on Its Shape."

The longer Mercator thought about his *Atlas*, the

bigger it became. It would be in several sections. The first part would tell the story of the creation of the world. Other parts would explain astronomy and the physical world. Finally, there would be more than 100 maps, bound in book form.

Mercator worked on many parts at once, publishing each section as it was completed. The first volume,

A map of North America and South America appeard in Mercator's Atlas.

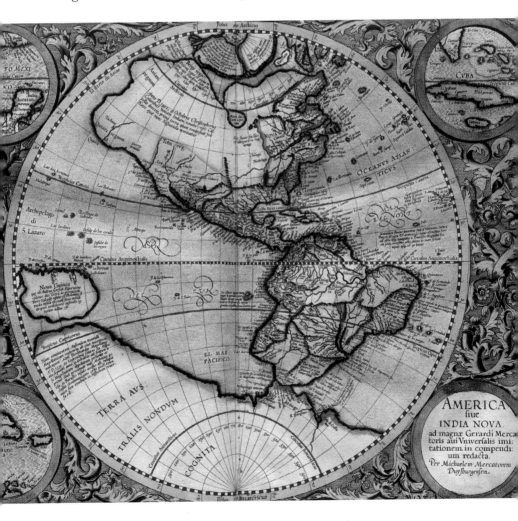

In ancient Greek mythology, Atlas was one of the super-beings called Titans. He took part in a war against the god Zeus. As a punishment, he had to carry the world on his shoulders. Atlas' mythical descendant, also named Atlas, was a king of the African land of Mauritania. This Atlas was a philosopher and scientist. Mercator claimed to be following in Atlas' footsteps as he compiled his map collection.

published in 1585, contained 51 maps. This was a good start, but tragedy struck as he continued to work. His wife, Barbara, and son Arnold both died over the next two years. Yet Mercator labored on. In 1589, he married Gertrude Vierlings, the widow of a wealthy friend, and his son Rumold married Gertrude's daughter. The second volume of the *Atlas*, with 23 more maps, appeared that same year.

The following year, at age 78, Mercator suffered a stroke. It paralyzed the left side of his body, and he had to be carried around the house in a chair. Much of the *Atlas* was yet to be finished. But nothing was more important to him than his account of the creation. It would provide a framework for everything else in the collection. As he wrote to a friend:

> Although this is the last part of my work, it will nonetheless be the most important, indeed the very base and summit of the whole. ... This will be the goal of all my labour, this will mark the end of my work.

Mercator knew that death was near. By now he could hardly hold a pen, and he was almost blind. Grappling with his disabilities, he struggled to complete the creation story. It was all for the glory of God, as he stated in the opening chapter:

> *For this is the main scope we aim at, that*
> *... the infinite wisdom of God, and his*
> *[inexhaustible] goodness, may be known*
> *... whereby we may be continually rapt up*
> *to reverence and honour his Majesty, & to*
> *embrace his rich goodness.*

Another stroke in 1593 left Mercator even more feeble. He knew he would not live to see the complete *Atlas* published. Although about 30 more maps were still in the works, he was satisfied. He had managed to finish what he believed was his finest work—an account of the creation of the world. On December 2, 1594, Gerardus Mercator died of a cerebral hemorrhage at the age of 82. As a friend wrote, he died "about mid-day, sitting in his chair before the hearth, as though dropping off to sleep."

In the spring of 1595, Mercator's son Rumold published the final volume of maps. Mercator's grandsons brought out another edition of the *Atlas* in 1602. But sales were not good, and they were running out of money. So they sold the engraved plates of the *Atlas* to the printer Jodocus Hondius. In 1606, Hondius

GERARDUS MERCATOR NATUS | IUDOCUS HONDIUS NATUS IN
RUPELMUNDÆ.III NON.MARTII ANNO | PAGO FLANDRIÆ.DICTO WACKENE XVI
CIƆIƆXII·VIXIT ANN.LXXXII.M.VIII.D. | KALEND.NOVEMBRIS ANNO CIƆIƆLXIII:
XXVI:DENATUS IV NON.DECEMBRIS | VIXIT ANN.XLVII.M.VII.D.XXIX:DENAT:
ANNO CIƆIƆXCIV. | US XIV KAL.MARTII ANNO CIƆIƆCXII.

An early 17th- century print depicts Gerardus Mercator with the printer Jodocus Hondius.

published a new edition—including the creation story and additional maps—but with Mercator's name still on the title page.

Hondius knew how to boost sales. He issued the *Atlas* in several languages, as well as a pocket-sized version. It sold in huge quantities. Other publishers imitated Hondius' success, and more map books flooded the market—all carrying the name *Atlas*.

Although he came up with the name *Atlas* that is used for books of maps to this day, Gerardus Mercator remains best known for his famous map projection. Over the years, Mercator projections have guided voyagers by land, sea, air, and space. Still, several mapmakers have tried making new maps with different projections, hoping to correct the distortions of Mercator's map. Geographer Arthur Robinson issued a new map in 1963. Like all mapmakers, he realized that no map could show accurate sizes, shapes, and distances all at once. So he used computer calculations to make the map as realistic as possible.

An image collected by NASA's Earth Observatory shows the Robinson projection.

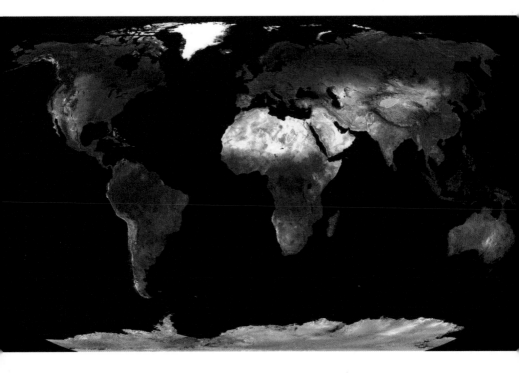

The German historian Arno Peters tried a new map, too. Peters' concerns were political and social. He felt that Mercator made developed countries look larger and more important than Third World countries. Peters introduced a new projection map

Mercator is honored by a statue in front of the town hall in Duisburg, Germany.

in 1973. He claimed it represented the areas of countries accurately.

But Peters' map had its drawbacks as well. It made Africa and South America look long and thin. Robinson said the map's landmasses looked like "wet, ragged, long winter underwear hung out to dry on the Arctic Circle." Still, many organizations adopted it as an alternative to Mercator's version. Many other maps appeared, each with strong and weak points.

Mercator's map may not be all things to all people. But in making it, his main concern had been the welfare of navigators. Today he would be pleased to know that almost all maps for navigation at sea use the Mercator projection.

So a map projection invented 450 years ago continues to guide cruise ships, jet planes, and space shuttles in the 21st century. It is truly an impressive legacy for the son of a poor shoemaker. ⮡

MERCATOR'S LIFE

1512

Born March 5 in Rupelmonde, Flanders (now in Belgium)

1527

Enrolls in the Brethren of the Common Life school in 's-Hertogenbosch (now in the Netherlands)

1532

Receives a degree from the University of Louvain

1515

1517

The first Spanish conquistadors, under Francisco Hernandez de Cordoba, reach the Yucatan Peninsula

1525

Spanish mapmaker Diego Ribeiro makes the first scientific charts of the Pacific Ocean

1531

The "great comet," later called Halley's Comet, causes a wave of superstition

WORLD EVENTS

1537

Produces his first map, a map of Palestine

1538

Produces his first map of the world, the first to show North and South America

1536

Marries Barbara Schelleken

1535

1539

Spanish explorer Hernando de Soto lands in Florida and claims it for Spain

1534

England's King Henry VIII passes the Act of Supremacy, declaring himself the head of the Church of England and breaking away from the Roman Catholic Church

MERCATOR'S LIFE

1540

Makes a map
of Flanders

1541

Makes a globe of the
world that's the first
to show rhumb lines

1544

Arrested for heresy
and imprisoned for
seven months

1540

1540

Spanish explorer
Francisco Vasquez de
Coronado leads an
expedition into what
is now the southwest-
ern United States

1541

Pedro de Valvidia
founds Santiago, Chile

1544

Pope Paul III opens
the Council of Trent

WORLD EVENTS

1545

Workshop receives
Emperor Charles V's
imperial seal
of approval

1552

Moves to Duisburg in
the duchy of Cleves
(now in Germany)

1554

Publishes a map
of Europe

1550

1545

The Catholic Counter-
Reformation begins
in Europe

1555

Artist Michelangelo
completes his
Pietà sculpture in
Florence, Italy

MERCATOR'S LIFE

1564
Appointed court cosmographer to Duke Wilhelm of Cleves

1568
Publishes his *Chronologia*, a history of the universe

1569
Publishes his famous world map for navigators, using the Mercator projection

1565

1564
Poet and playwright William Shakespeare is born

1570
The potato is introduced to Europe from South America

WORLD EVENTS

1589

Publishes the
second volume
of *Atlas;* marries
Gertrude Vierlings

1594

Dies December 2 at
age 82 in Duisburg

1578

Publishes a
corrected version
of Ptolemy's maps

1577

Francis Drake sails
around the world by
way of Cape Horn

1589

Galileo Galilei
becomes professor
of mathematics at the
University of Pisa

1592

Trinity College,
Ireland's oldest
university, is
founded in Dublin

DATE OF BIRTH: March 5, 1512

BIRTHPLACE: Rupelmonde, Flanders (now in Belgium)

FATHER: Hubert Kremer (?–1526)

MOTHER: Emerentia Kremer (?–c. 1529)

EDUCATION: University of Louvain, master's degree

FIRST SPOUSE: Barbara Schelleken (?–1586)

DATE OF MARRIAGE: August 1536

CHILDREN: Arnold (1537–1587)
Emerentia (1538–1567)
Dorothée (1539–1578)
Bartholomew (1540–1568)
Rumold (c. 1541– c. 1600)
Katharina (c. 1542–?)

SECOND SPOUSE: Gertrude Vierlings (?–?)

DATE OF MARRIAGE: September 1589

DATE OF DEATH: December 2, 1594

PLACE OF BURIAL: St. Saviour's Church, Duisburg

FURTHER READING

Billings, Henry. *Maps, Globes, Graphs.* Austin, Texas: Steck-Vaughn, 2004.

Chancellor, Deborah. *Maps and Mapping.* New York: Kingfisher, 2004.

Johnson, Sylvia A. *Mapping the World.* New York: Atheneum Books, 1999.

Oleksy, Walter G. *Maps in History.* New York: Franklin Watts, 2002.

Sammis, Fran. *Maps and Mapmaking.* Tarrytown, N.Y.: Benchmark Books, 2000.

Smith, A. G. *Where Am I?: The Story of Maps and Navigation.* Toronto, Canada: Stoddart Kids, 1997.

Wolfman, Ira. *My World and Globe.* Rev. ed. New York: Workman Pub., 2003.

LOOK FOR MORE SIGNATURE LIVES
BOOKS ABOUT THIS ERA:

Tycho Brahe: *Pioneer of Astronomy*

Nicolaus Copernicus: *Father of Modern Astronomy*

Galileo: *Astronomer and Physicist*

Robert Hooke: *Natural Philosopher and Scientific Explorer*

Sir Isaac Newton: *Brilliant Mathematician and Scientist*

On the Web

For more information on this topic,
use FactHound.

1. Go to *www.facthound.com*
2. Type in this book ID: 0756533120
3. Click on the *Fetch It* button.

FactHound will fetch the best
Web sites for you.

Historic Sites

Osher Map Library and Smith Center for
Cartographic Education
University of Southern Maine
314 Forest Ave.
Portland, ME 04104
207/780-4850
Original maps, atlases, and globes dating
from 1475

The Mariners' Museum
100 Museum Drive
Newport News, VA 23606
757/596-2222
Early maps, navigation instruments, model
ships, and other artifacts from the Age of
Exploration to today

calligrapher
expert in formal, decorative handwriting

cartography
mapmaking

cosmographer
person responsible for making maps based
on astronomical observations

heresy
beliefs that are contrary to established
religious doctrine

heretic
someone who is guilty of heresy

humanism
a philosophy that favors learning by observation
and logic rather than accepting information based
on faith

navigators
people who steer and manage a ship's course

papier-mâché
mixture of paper and glue that hardens when dry

philosophy
study of logic, ethics, and natural laws to
achieve wisdom

projection
method of representing the curved Earth on a
flat surface

rhumb lines
lines drawn across the oceans from one land point
to another that show the direction a ship would
sail if it followed its compass on a constant course

surveyors
people who measure distances and angles in order
to map land features

Chapter 1

Page 10, line 2: Walter Ghim. *Vita Mercatoris*. Trans. A. S. Osley in *Mercator: A Monograph on the Lettering of Maps, etc. in the 16th Century Netherlands with a Facsimile and Translation of His Treatise on the Italic Hand and a Translation of Ghim's Vita Mercatoris*. London: Faber & Faber, 1969, p. 190.

Chapter 3

Page 25, line 20: Ibid., p. 47.

Chapter 4

Page 31, line 13: Ibid., p. 39.

Page 33, line 18: Nicholas Crane. *Mercator: The Man Who Mapped the Planet*, New York: Henry Holt and Company, 2002, p. 41.

Page 35, line 4: Andrew Taylor. *The World of Gerard Mercator: The Mapmaker Who Revolutionized Geography*. New York: Walker & Company, 2004, p. 66.

Page 35, line 18: Ibid., p. 58.

Page 37, line 6: *Mercator: The Man Who Mapped the Planet*, p. 44.

Chapter 5

Page 42, line 1: *Vita Mercatoris*, p. 185.

Page 42, line 21: A. S. Osley. *Mercator: A Monograph on the Lettering of Maps*, p. 20.

Page 44, line 22: *Mercator: The Man Who Mapped the Planet*, p. 66.

Page 46, line 20: *The World of Gerard Mercator: The Mapmaker Who Revolutionized Geography*, p. 78.

Page 47, line 5: *Mercator: A Monograph on the Lettering of Maps*, pp. 20–21.

Chapter 6

Page 50, line 10: *Vita Mercatoris*, p. 190.

Chapter 7

Page 62, line 10: *Mercator: A Monograph on the Lettering of Maps*, p. 21.

Page 64, line 2: *The World of Gerard Mercator: The Mapmaker Who Revolutionized Geography*, p. 110.

Page 64, line 10: Ibid., p. 111.

Page 64, line 16: *Mercator: The Man Who Mapped the Planet*, p. 139.

Page 65, line 9: *The World of Gerard Mercator: The Mapmaker Who Revolutionized Geography*, p. 116.

Chapter 8

Page 70, line 5: *Vita Mercatoris*, pp. 186–187.

Page 71, line 7: Ibid., p. 187.

Page 73, line 8: Ibid., p. 190.

Page 73, line 25: "Gerardus Mercator: A Famous Cartographer in Duisburg." *Duisport*. December 2005, p. 33. 21 July 2006. www.duisport.de/en/duisport_gruppe/aktuelles_archiv/duisport_magazin/pdf/december_2005_en.pdf

Page 75, line 14: Ibid., p. 33

Page 76, line 2: *Vita Mercatoris*, p. 189.

Chapter 9

Page 79, line 11: Eli Maor. "A Mapmaker's Paradise." *Trigonometric Delights*. Princeton, N.J.: Princeton University Press, 2002, pp. 170–171. 22 July 2006, www.pupress.princeton.edu/books/maor/chapter_13.pdf

Page 80, line 2: "Gipsy Moth IV (Sir Francis Chichester): A National Maritime Heritage Treasure." 25 August 2006. www.gipsymoth.org/man_leg04_main.asp

Page 83, line 19: "Gerardus Mercator." MostlyMaps.com 9 May 2007. www.mostlymaps.com/reference/Map-Makers/gerardus-mercator.php

Page 85, line 5: Elial F. Hall. "Gerard Mercator: His Life and Works." *Journal of the American Geographical Society of New York* 10.4 (1878), p. 184.

Chapter 10

Page 88, line 13: *Mercator: The Man Who Mapped the Planet*, p. 213.

Page 90, line 23: Ibid., p. 282.

Page 91, line 6: Gerardus Mercator. *Atlas or A geographicke description of the regions, countries and kingdomes of the world, through Europe, Asia, Africa, and America, represented by new & exact maps.* Trans. Henry Hexham. Amsterdam: Henry Hondius and Iohn Iohnson, 1626, p. 1. 23 July 2006. http://gateway.proquest.com/openurl?ctx_ver=Z39.88-2003&res_id=xri:eebo&rft_val_fmt=&rft_id=xri:eebo:image:23179

Page 91, line 20: *Mercator: A Monograph on the Lettering of Maps*, p. 194.

Page 95, line 5: Arthur Robinson. "Arno Peters and His New Cartography." *The American Cartographer.* October 1985. Quoted in John P. Snyder, "Social Consciousness and World Maps." 28 August 2006. www.religion-online.org/showarticle.asp?title=976

Alexander, James. "Loxodromes: A Rhumb Way to Go." *Mathematics Magazine* 77.5 (2004), pp. 349–356. 19 July 2006. www.cwru.edu/artsci/math/alexander/mathmag349–356.pdf

Crane, Nicholas. *Mercator: The Man Who Mapped the Planet.* New York: Henry Holt and Company, 2002.

"Gerardus Mercator: A Famous Cartographer in Duisburg." *Duisport.* December 2005, pp. 32–33. 21 July 2006. www.duisport.de/en/duisport_gruppe/aktuelles_archiv/duisport_magazin/pdf/december_2005_en.pdf

"Gipsy Moth IV (Sir Francis Chichester): A National Maritime Heritage Treasure." 25 August 2006. www.gipsymoth.org/man_leg04_main.asp

Hall, Elial F. "Gerard Mercator: His Life and Works." *Journal of the American Geographical Society of New York* 10.4 (1878), pp. 163–196.

Jansen, Eelco. "Catholic Book Censorship in the 16th century Netherlands." *Journal of the XVth Annual ISHA Conference, Pula 2004*, pp. 13–18. Pula, Croatia: 2005. 10 August 2006. www.isha-international.org/download/journals/Journl%20Pula%202004.doc

Maor, Eli. "A Mapmaker's Paradise." *Trigonometric Delights.* Princeton, N.J.: Princeton University Press, 2002, pp. 165–180. 22 July 2006. www.pupress.princeton.edu/books/maor/chapter_13.pdf

"Mapping Toolbox." *The MathWorks: MATLAB and Simulink for Technical Computing.* 2006. 21 July 2006. www.mathworks.com

"Mercator." 10 August 2006. http://mathsforeurope.digibel.be/mercator.htm

Mercator, Gerardus. *Atlas or A geographicke description of the regions, countries and kingdomes of the world, through Europe, Asia, Africa, and America, represented by new & exact maps.* Trans. Henry Hexham. Amsterdam: Henry Hondius and Iohn Iohnson, 1626. 23 July 2006. http://gateway.proquest.com/openurl?ctx_ver=Z39.88-2003&res_id=xri:eebo&rft_val_fmt=&rft_id=xri:eebo:image:23179

Monmonier, Mark. *Rhumb Lines and Map Wars: A Social History of the Mercator Projection.* Chicago: University of Chicago Press, 2004.

O'Connor, John J., and Edmund F. Robertson. "Gerardus Mercator." *The MacTutor History of Mathematics.* 19 July 2006. www-history.mcs.st-andrews.ac.uk/Biographies/Mercator_Gerardus.html

Osley, A. S. *Mercator: A Monograph on the Lettering of Maps, etc. in the 16th Century Netherlands with a Facsimile and Translation of His Treatise on the Italic Hand and a Translation of Ghim's Vita Mercatoris.* London: Faber & Faber, 1969.

Ritter, Michael E. "Locational Systems: Latitude and Longitude." *The Physical Environment: An Introduction to Physical Geography.* 2006. 21 July 2006. www.uwsp.edu/geo/faculty/ritter/geog101/textbook/essentials/locational_systems.html

Robinson, Arthur. "Arno Peters and His New Cartography." *The American Cartographer,* October 1985. Quoted by John P. Snyder, "Social Consciousness and World Maps." 28 August 2006. http://www.religion-online.org/showarticle.asp?title=976

Rosenberg, Matt. "Peters Projection vs. Mercator Projection." 21 July 2006. http://geography.about.com/library/weekly/aa030201a.htm

Taylor, Andrew. *The World of Gerard Mercator: The Mapmaker Who Revolutionized Geography.* New York: Walker & Company, 2004.

Ann Heinrichs is the author of more than 200 books for children and young adults. Her favorite subjects are geography and history. An avid traveler, Ann has journeyed through the Middle East, Africa, and the Far East, as well as Europe and the United States. An amateur map collector, she has also studied navigation. Using Mercator projections, she has steered sailboats along a compass course—and reached her destination.

Image Credits